WALKING IN THE
Supernatural

A story of Hope in trying time

Victoria Owen

Kingdom Publishers

Walking in the Supernatural
A story of Hope in trying time

Copyright© Victoria Owen

All rights reserved. No part of this book may be
reproduced in any form by photocopying or any
electronic or mechanical means, including information
storage or retrieval systems, without permission in
writing from both the copyright owner and the publisher
of the book. The right of Jennifer Muthoni to be identified as the author of
this work has been asserted by her in
accordance with the Copyright, Designs and Patents Act
1988 and any subsequent amendments thereto.
A catalogue record for this book is available from the
British Library.

All Scripture Quotations have been taken from the New International Version and the
King James Version of the Bible.

ISBN: 978-1-911697-44-2

1st Edition by Kingdom Publishers
Kingdom Publishers
London, UK.

You can purchase copies of this book from any leading bookstore or email
contact@kingdompublishers.co.uk

Table of Contents

Introduction	5
CHAPTER 1: *The Gift*	9
CHAPTER 2: *The Encounters*	19
CHAPTER 3: *The Accident in the Valleys*	27
CHAPTER 4: *The Oppression*	37
CHAPTER 5: *The Coronavirus Siege*	49
CHAPTER 6: *Prophetic Healing*	57
CHAPTER 7: *The Future*	63
CHAPTER 8: *You Too Can Receive This Experience*	73
Conclusion	85
Dedication	89

Introduction

Walking in the Supernatural is an overwhelming and emotional story of Mwape and how God is still in our everyday life and it is also about how You also can live in this supernatural life. The bible says, "For who hath despised the day of small things?" (Zechariah 4:10a) and in the book of Luke we see the Lord Jesus encouraging young people to come to Him, as he said "But Jesus called them unto him, and said, suffer little children to come unto me, and forbid them not: for of such is the kingdom of God. Verily I say unto you, whosoever shall not receive the kingdom of God as a little child shall in no wise enter therein." (Luke 18:16

Mwape learned how to build her relationship with God through prayers from her early childhood days, altering everything about her. Her walk with God birthed so many things for her - from an explosive prayer life to a growing faith and mysterious heavenly encounters - her experience was phenomenal! Her relationship with God taught her to depend on Him in every situation. Hence why when her family came down with the destructive impact of Coronavirus, Mwape did what she new best, she ran to the Lord. In the heat of a powerful prayer session, she was set aflame by the Holy Spirit. Her husband, unaware of what was happening, touched her and instantly felt a wave of God's power coursing through him, and

He was immediately healed. It seemed like one of the happiest days of their lives until a few days later

****

From her story, you will also learn how to build your relationship with God so that you too can navigate the formidable challenges of life without fear or disbelief. More than anything you'll ever need in life, this book will stir up your spirit and awaken your spiritual consciousness that we live in the last days, characterized by the evil signs we are witnessing today - one of which is the ravaging coronavirus pandemic that is destroying lives today. Thus, the need to prepare for the great day of the Lord.

In a world faced with so many harsh realities, there has never been a time when it has become so crucial for people to draw closer to God. The reason is not far-fetched. Science can fail. Education can fail. Technology can fail. Everything can fail. One thing that will still stand the test of time is the Omnipotent, Omnipresent, and Omniscient personality of God and his Word. He remains unchangeable throughout time and ages!

Sadly, many people have become too busy to understand this truth that when everything else fails, we should never forget to turn to God for answers to our problems. He shouldn't be our alternative. He has always been our ULTIMATE SOLUTION, but we've been blinded by worldly allurements that we don't even notice His importance. We also fail to teach our children and our younger ones the value of being close to God through an effective prayer life. So when they grow up, they do not know Him or His power because they have been trained to trust in their skills, talents, abilities, resources, wealth, and other superficial things more than they trust and have faith in God.

Unfortunately, the people who died during the Coronavirus pandemic's siege had all these amazing qualities, too, probably even more. But as we speak, there are over 2 million great talents, potentials, and persons of influence lying six feet below the ground. And perhaps they never even had the slightest opportunity to say goodbye to their loved ones. But none of that matters now. The major concern, which should bother us all, is where these millions of lost souls will spend eternity after exiting the earth with the horrifying experience of Covid-19. It proves just how brief life can be and why it is essential to check our priorities to align with our earthly and eternal goals.

I assure you that this book will bring you all the answers you need, dispel your fears about the Covid-19 virus, and equip you with the revelational solution that worked for Mwape and her family. More importantly, it will draw you closer to God in preparation for the imminent return of our Lord Jesus Christ.

You will find this book entertaining, enlightening, inspiring, and thought-provoking. However, you will gain the most from reading this book and practising everything that has been shared therein. I guarantee you that this book will transform your life in more ways than you can ever imagine, physically, Emotionally, and Spiritually. This book aims not to show you that there is hope in Covid-19 only but also for all of life's situations.

Happy reading!

CHAPTER ONE

The Gift

On the Southern part of the continent of Africa lies a fairly large country estimated to be about three times the size of the United Kingdom. The country is characterized by its abundant natural resources and its tropical weather conditions. During the dry season, it can be really hot, and when the rain comes, it brings violent thunderstorms so loud you fear the skies might come apart in an instant. Nevertheless, the wildlife adventures, waterfalls, and fun moments with other children and neighbours are priceless and something to always look forward to.

The experience is something you don't ever want to leave behind because, as they say, there is no place like home. It was here in Zambia that Mwape had her formative years. If there were one thing any child would long for, it would be an atmosphere of camaraderie ignited by the love, care, affection, and sense of responsibility exuding from the blissful love of one's parents. But this wasn't to be in her case because her life was filled with crevices that filtered in negative energy that caused her parents to drift apart.

Her father left when she was very young, abandoning her distraught mother to raise six children all by herself. But that was only the beginning of many "interesting" experiences to come.

Mom didn't have it easy. The pressure of letting go of marriage as a Christian woman and the responsibilities that followed in raising six children all by herself was just too much to bear. Luckily, her whole family waded in to help raise the kids. At least, as much as they could offer. Despite the additional help, it was still a significant burden that overwhelmed her because Mom had no other choice than to shoulder all the responsibilities since her parents were elderly and didn't have the energy they used to.

To reduce the stress on their elderly grandparents, Mwape and some of her siblings took up menial jobs near their home to support the family. Nevertheless, it was still quite a surprise to see how Mom found such magnanimous strength despite the overwhelming challenges. Mom did her best to be a perfect mother. She ventured into many businesses to educate and build her family a home, which she eventually did.

If there was one thing that kept her mother going during those trying moments, it was her relationship with God and her reckless faith in Him. It was with the same Godly standards that she raised all her children. Her mother was there for them, providing the needed guidance, counsel, and training, as much as she could so that all her children could lead better lives.

During Mwape's early childhood days, about 76% of Zambia's population were Protestants. The remaining 24% were Roman Catholic, Muslim Buddhist, Hindu, etc. But the religious atmosphere for Christians changed with the emergence of the Pentecostal and Charismatic movement that began about two decades ago. The supernatural move of God's awesome power saw a rise in faith and more people coming to terms with God's true knowledge and understanding. Mom had caught the revival, too, and was determined to dedicate all she had to God.

This is why despite the tons of challenges on her hands, she still managed to maintain a powerful faith in God. And she made sure she passed on those spiritual tenets onto her six children. In fact, one of her favourite scriptural passages is in Proverbs 22:6, which says, "Train up a child in the way he should go, And when he is old, he will not depart from it."

Mom started imparting spiritual values to her children at a very young age. She taught them to pray, read and understand the bible, and worship God appropriately. Despite all the lessons and warnings, it didn't stop their youthful exuberance. Still, God was merciful. Mom's relationship with God had blossomed to the point that she started manifesting unusual gifts, including prophecies, prayers, and declarations that often left people astounded. As one of the fellowship leaders, she was always busy with other church members praying and sharing the word of God.

Mom was actively doing God's work, and she underestimated God's plan for her family. As it later turned out, God wanted to release a trans-generational gift upon her family. The first proof was when Mwape's elder brother started manifesting the prophetic gift, too, making him the second in the family to have such an unusual ability. He would also get visions and foretell events before they happened. Mwape, on the other hand, was yet to discover her place in this generational family mandate. She only knew the Lord by name but not on a deeper, personal level.

If any quality made Mwape stand out, it was her verbosity and audacity - a characteristic that one could easily be mistaken for stubbornness or arrogance. But she was just a self-opinionated young girl who wouldn't capitulate to negative situations just because she wouldn't put up a fight.

Mwape grew up in a town that was notorious for one particular evil - kidnapping little children, killing them, and harvesting their organs for sale. Their strategy was very simple. They approach the children in a friendly, familiar way, offering them sweets and other lovely things that children naturally crave. The children, unsuspecting and naive, would fall into this trap until they are whisked away to be hacked into pieces. And afterwards, their innocent, fragile body parts would be offered for sale or be devoured by soul-less advocates of the Devil who satisfy their cravings with flesh and blood.

One sultry afternoon, her little sister was playing around the house. Suddenly, a young man emerged from nowhere, cautiously surveying the environment. When he felt the coast was clear, he whisked her sister over her shoulders, ready to run. Luckily, Mwape was close enough to see all that happened. She knew that if she did nothing and the young man succeeded, that would be the last time she'd set her eyes on her little sister. But that was not the only problem. No other person was around. So, without wasting time, she quickly improvised. She wore a fabric on her head to look like her mother and to look more mature. She climbed onto something that made her figure tower above the wall fence. Mwape blurted out loudly, "Hey you! Put that girl down or else…" The young man, caught off-guard, dropped her sister and took to his heels as fast as he could. It was then she realized that she was endowed with the spirit of boldness.

Soon after that incident, another one happened. Once again, the children were playing together around their houses, happy and cheerful as usual. Unfortunately, the moment was shortlived. The kidnappers had shown up again, this time with a different strategy. They came with dogs to scare everyone away, especially the little children. Their plan worked because as soon as they showed up, everyone scampered for safety, hiding away in their houses. Anyone who lagged was caught, captured, and taken to the slaughterhouse to have their organs harvested.

Then Mwape, along with the others, ran when she suddenly remembered something. She stopped short in her tracks, looking behind for her younger brother, who was a twin. She quickly retraced her steps to where he could have been. By this time, the kidnappers were closing upon him fast. Luckily, she made it in time to the spot before her brother was captured. As she arrived at the scene, she came face to face with the criminals. But she didn't run this time. Instead, she decided to confront them at once. She stood before them, giving the intruder a long, penetrating gaze. It looked as though she was enchanting him and his dog. And for a brief moment, they stood helpless. She bent over and picked up her little brother unscathed, and went home.

The incident began to replay in Mwape's mind again. She wondered how these things usually worked out in her favour, but she couldn't tell what it was. At first, she concluded it was because of her verbosity. But obviously, it wasn't because of her mouth because it got her into trouble a lot, and she ended up being beaten. So, there was more to her gift than meets the eye. She'd have to find out one way or another.

Many years later, during her boarding school days in secondary school, she became sick. However, the cause of her illness could not be ascertained. Whenever she hung out with her friends or visited the hospital, as long as she was outdoors, she suddenly felt better, and the symptoms of her illness vanished. As soon as she returned to her hostel room and laid on her bed, she started to feel unwell again.

One day, she was alone during leisure time, relaxing. Her friend, who hadn't seen her in a short while, bumped into her and said, "Hi! I heard you haven't been feeling well." She looked worried. "What's wrong?" Mwape explained the situation to her friend, who looked surprised. "What? Are you sure someone has not bewitched your bed?" For a moment, her friend seemed to make a lot of sense, and it stirred something within her. But the question was, why would anyone want to do that to her?

During this time, Mwape was not yet a Pentecostal Christian who understood the power in the name of Jesus. Her highest point in faith was in her parents and grandparents. So, she went back to her hostel after discussing it with her friend. As she entered the room, she hesitated a moment. She looked inquiringly at her bed, her eyes scanning every length and breadth of it, as though she was hoping she'd find something. There was no other person in the room with her.

Steadying her gaze on the bed now after all her roommates came in after dinner, Mwape stood on top of a bunk bed and started addressing her roommates, saying, "Hey! Listen. I don't know who has done something to my bed that is messing with my health. I don't care if you're a witch or whatever. Just take out whatever you've put on my bed now because I'll call my dead grandparents who will come after you and severely punish you and everyone close to you for what you're doing to me."

Funnily, her grandparents were perfectly fine at the time. Again, it was just her mouth making bold utterances in a bid to allay her fears. But did it work? Well, shortly after that, the girl staying directly under her bed left the school, but she didn't say if she was responsible or not. The only noticeable thing was that after class the next day, all her things were gone, and she was nowhere to be found. Mwape's health was restored.

As Mwape grew in faith, she became more prayerful. This made her more connected to God, and she began to see things. Only this time, her vision came with a form of darkness in her view. She started seeing deaths, whether through suicides or natural deaths, before they even occurred in waking life. To imagine that her first experience with her visions was negative imagery scared the life out of her.

And to make it worse, three deaths happened shortly after these visions - her friend's sister, a teacher, and a young boy she had become acquainted with for a short time. The boy had caused her trouble in the past, so she had told him that they were better off as distant friends. His death seemed to be the most painful for her, messing her up mentally and making her feel guilty each time she remembered it. She kept blaming herself, thinking if only she had continued to be his friend, he could have opened up to her about what he was going through.

Shortly after that, her auntie died too, and she became more confused, unhappy, and angry at God, whom she trusted to see her through. It seemed as though some people blamed her first for not looking out for a friend, and secondly, for not being helping her aunt more, even though she died from tuberculosis complications.

Life was more complicated than she had thought. With her mother living far away in the UK and her estranged father who hardly visited nor thought about them, and with a home that didn't quite feel like home, nothing seemed to make sense anymore.

One of her friends noticed how sullen she looked and introduced her to drinking, assuring her that it would make her feel great again. And as her friend promised, it happened just like that. Indeed, she began to regain her youthful glow again. Liquor became her best companion, and the clubs were just another home where she longed to be, one she'd gladly visit anytime. It eased her pain and made her feel comfortable in the most fantastic way.

One day, Mwape and her friend Racheal decided to go to church for Carol service, at a Catholic church and on their way, they decided to buy some bottles of alcohol and drunk while walking to church, suddenly, a Heavy thunderous stormy Rain came gashing down with lighting to a point, the two of them feared God was going to punish them, with that in mind, they started throwing away the bottles of alcohol thinking God would kill them with lightening for being Naughty and repented. But just when they survived the stormy Rain the following day like many people do, they forgot about the promise they made to God to stop sinning, and for Mwape indirectly, She just wanted to punish God for not saving her aunty when she prayed for her not to die. She wanted Him to feel what she felt. She believed He had abandoned her amid all the troubles she'd been going through. With everyone blaming her for all the misfortunes that were happening, God was certainly the last person she wanted to talk to.

About four years later, she arrived in the UK. Mom had planned for her to come and continue her education there. At least, they'd be close to each other there, and Mom could take care of her. At first, the change in the environment had little or no effect on her character as she continued her drinking spree. Luckily for her, drinks were very cheap in that part of the world. She could drink any time of the day because drinking made her feel safe, happy and made her forget all her worries.

As she carried on living this type of life, it was as though she was digging her own pit. She noticed that although she was trying to get back at God, it was really difficult for her. And as the days went by, she felt so lost in herself. Then one day, she saw some policemen parked in the neighbourhood. Overpowered by the battle that raged within her, she suddenly felt like screaming to them for help but lost her voice. Then she realized that what she struggled with was not just physical, and no one could save her from the storm bottled within her. She thought about reaching out to someone stronger than her for help, but she didn't have the courage to do that. And with that, she carried on drinking to the point of addiction.

Chapter Summary

Family is an important component of any society that should not be taken for granted.

Parents have a great responsibility in the training and development of their children.

When you train your children in the way of the Lord, it's one of the best investments you can make in life.

As parents, you should be involved in your children's lives. They'll always need direction and guidance.

The foundation of a child's upbringing is as important as his future. How are you training your children?

In the next chapter, you will learn...

Why it is important not just to know the Lord but also to have a great relationship with Him.

The Lord still wants you no matter how bad you feel about yourself. Just surrender.

If you want the Lord to use you, make yourself available to Him.

CHAPTER TWO

The Encounters

Many days just went by, but this particular one was different. It was the day Mwape decided to take stock of her life and reflect on some of her actions and decisions. As she sat in the corner of her room reminiscing about her past adventures and escapades, she thought to herself that she'd be wasting her life if she continued living this way.

So, she decided to take her schooling seriously. However, settling down in college in a foreign institution came with its own challenges too. Learning was difficult for her as the accent would take some getting used to, and the teachers needed to slow down a little when speaking so she could understand.

On the other end of the rope, her fellow students scorned her for almost every mistake she made. For that reason, she hated being in the United Kingdom. The thought of remaining there conjured an ill-feeling of loneliness that made her think of returning to her country where she belonged. If that were what green pastures felt or looked like on the other side of the Mediterranean, she'd prefer to stay in Zambia, where home really was, along with the rich culture, robust heritage, and warm ambience it offered. But since living in the UK had some advantages, too, so she decided change her mind-set and worked hard until she was finally able to balance her spiritual, social, and academic life.

Sometime in 2009, after a long struggle internally, her friend invited her to a church conference that felt like home for the first time since she'd arrived in the UK. But that was not enough to convince her to stop clubbing, fornicating, drinking, etc. Then one fateful day, she received a letter from an unknown source.

As she opened it, the opening paragraph read, "My daughter..." That took her back briefly. Mom didn't call her that, and Dad had not been in contact, nor was he very affectionate. She held tightly to the mysterious letter, scanning its entire contents as she wondered who could have sent or written it. As she read, she was shocked to realize that the writer knew about her delinquent behaviour and spared nothing in mentioning all of them in the letter. However, in closing, it was wrapped up with several scriptural promises of honour, restoration, and favour that could be hers if only she gave up her wayward lifestyle and turned to the Lord for help. Soon after receiving the message, she lost it and never found the letter again despite her efforts to recover it.

She couldn't help but wonder if the AUTHOR and the FINISHER of the letter was the leader of the faith Himself! This was an act that defies human logic and wisdom, no matter the interpretation. Based on this idea, she dropped to her knees and pleaded for mercy. "Lord, I know who I am. I am empty. I've been a failure. And all my life, I've been blamed for everything bad that has happened. Now, if you can take these unpleasant circumstances in my life and turn them into something beautiful even at the risk of me not following through because I'm definitely not the best, then I'm yours."

In that instant, the Devil began to speak, countering the Lord's offer and telling her she was about to make a wrong choice. He tried to make her believe that she was on the verge of losing a wild, youthful, and adventurous life where everything seemed so easy and fun-filled. But before she could succumb to the alluring words of the Devil, the Lord spoke again, "If you don't become born again, many people will go to hell because of you."

Considering the enormity of the responsibility, she could have rescinded, but for the sake of the lives that would pay for her refusal, she accepted the Lord's offer on the condition that He help her to work on her weaknesses. And from that moment, her life was never the same. Her prayer and bible study life improved tremendously. That was the beginning of the many encounters she had and the start of her youth ministry, which saw many young people giving their lives to Christ.

Of all the miracles she had witnessed, one readily strikes a chord in her heart. It was after one of her numerous youth conventions where the Spirit of the Lord had descended so heavily on the young people they were literally crying out to the Lord passionately in the total dedication of their lives to God.

On this fateful day, Mwape met with a friend who had a request. "I have a friend who is in the hospital. The doctor has given him just three days to live. Please come and pray for him." She agreed and immediately went over to see him. He was really in a bad situation, skinny, writhing in pain, and with no strength to keep fighting the venomous sting of cancer.

The days kept counting down, and his situation kept worsening. She'd been praying for him, but it appeared nothing was happening. The D-day had finally come, and everyone was eager to see the miracle that would take place. On that same day, he looked better. He even tried walking around. The progress seemed gradual but what was more remarkable was how greatly his health had improved. The tubes that were connected to his body were removed, and he even managed to eat a little. The miracle was real!

Then she had a vision. She saw the young boy looking perfectly healthy, glowing, talking, and smiling happily. She was happy to see him alive and well. As soon as she woke from the dream, she called one of her pastors, told him about the young boy, and they baptized him. That day, he gave his life to Christ. His friends and girlfriend, who had witnessed the miraculous recovery, gave their lives to Christ too on the spot.

Shortly after that, she revisited the young boy to pray for him. A few other people were around too. As she prayed, she felt the Spirit of the Lord resting heavily upon her. In that instant, she wanted to transfer power to the young boy so that his healing would be complete, but someone else had touched her. It was a family friend, the woman she fondly called "auntie," also diagnosed with cancer. And as soon as contact was made, Mwape's Auntie screamed, and her shriek filled the entire room. Immediately, she sensed that the virtue had gone out of her. As soon as that happened, the people around started praying. A few months later, she went in for a medical check-up, and to her greatest surprise, she was healed of cancer.

As Mwape relaxed one cool evening, the Lord came in a dream and explained the vision He had shown her earlier about the young boy. As it turned out, the Lord wanted her to prepare him for life in eternity by helping him become born again.

One particular night, exactly four months later, while Mwape was meditating, she was caught in a trance where she saw the boy. He looked perfectly healthy. As he drew closer, she could notice the transition. He looked more handsome and was basking in the glory of the Lord. But something was missing. It was the tone with which he spoke. It was a rather sober one, but she couldn't tell what it was. So, she listened to him as he calmly said to her, "Thank you so much for everything. Don't worry about me anymore. Don't try to do anything. I'm fine now."

The next day, her phone rang. It was the young boy's girlfriend who had called to inform her that he was dead. Upon hearing that, Mwape had no choice but to accept the Lord's decision and praise Him, knowing that the young boy was now resting in heaven.

On one particular occasion, she was led in the Spirit to tell a woman in church that the Lord would bless her with some cars. And it happened that way exactly one month later. She got her first car, and soon after, others followed. Someone came to her and said, "The Lord asked me to give you these car keys." However, the woman had a challenge with her sight, one of the reasons she'd been denied a license and other driving documents. So, her husband drove most of the time.

One Saturday after the women's conference, the woman prayed that God would heal her sight and help her read something from a distance. It was at that precise moment that the Lord revealed something about the woman with the poor sight. Immediately, Mwape prayed for her that the Lord grant her heart's desire. Instantly, she was healed, and she could read well.

Soon after that, the Lord showed her another woman. She was elegant, sophisticated, and charming. She had casually strolled into the church that morning. The woman wasn't in any particular church. She'd been going from denomination to denomination without solidly planting her feet in one. Just then, the Lord gave Mwape a message for the woman. "Go to that woman over there. She's been to many churches. Tell her I've heard her, and I've seen her."

At this time, the woman was about to leave the church while the service was still in session. On the directive of the Lord, Mwape addressed the woman by the door and delivered the message. The woman who appeared stunned looked at her and asked, "How did you know? That's all I ever asked the Lord to tell me - that He's seen me and He's heard me. Nothing more and nothing less." The woman's response taught Mwape a fundamental lesson - when God tells you two words, don't add a third.

With her numerous expressions of God's gift in her life, Mwape's popularity began to grow in church as people wanted to be prayed for or be ministered to by her. This soon created a rift between her and the church management team as she was advised to learn to follow protocol before ministering to anyone since she was still a novice. So, she obeyed, but that didn't stop her from doing whatever God led her to do.

As she continued to learn the ways of the Lord, she grew confident about God's plan for her life. And soon, God began to reveal more of His intentions for her future even though they didn't seem to make sense to her. She foresaw her future before it came to pass - her marriage, family, her suffering, the loss of a child, and the coming of the Lord.

She eventually got married to her husband, whom she led to the Lord with the help of the church family. Thankfully, he didn't have much to work on and became a Christian who loved the Lord as well. And, as it turned out, God had a special assignment for her husband too. The Lord overturned his weaknesses and aligned him with the right mentors who would help him become a useful vessel in God's hand. One day, her son told them he saw angels praying in tongues when they all had Covid-19. Surprisingly, he'd never been taught about angels. In that instant, it became more evident the purpose of God for her family and that her gift wasn't a curse after all.

As Mwape began to grow in her walk with God, she had many spiritual encounters, especially with visions and outofbody experiences that made it seem like she lived an everyday life. All of this culminated in an experience that further reinforced her spiritual growth. What once seemed like bad dreams were actually a call to action, proving to her that you only move forward in faith, not backwards.

Chapter Summary

The important thing in life is to give your life to Christ and become born again.

God does not give you a gift by accident. He gives it to you by His divine plan and requires you to express it, not hide it like the servants who hid their talents in the scriptures.

Don't ever add or subtract from the word of the Lord. There are dire consequences.

In walking with God, you will need fiery consecration. This will keep you burning for Him and an active prayer life; it increases your sensitivity to the Lord and what He wants you to do.

Sometimes, it's better to Trust God's plan over certain situations without asking questions because, like the bible says, He knows the end of all things from the beginning.

In the next chapter, you will learn...

Why it is important to trust God at all times and in all things.

Why obedience is essential in serving the Lord.

The Lord watches over us to protect us without us even knowing it.

CHAPTER THREE

The Accident in the Valleys

They were returning to the boarding school after an interschool competition when she heard a voice. It wasn't a familiar one, nor was it the voice of anyone around. She stopped short. She couldn't tell where the voice was coming from. It was like a thought coming through her mind, or so she thought. "Look at the tires," the voice said, so calm and reassuring. Immediately, her eyes opened, and she saw, as though in a vision, a vehicle with the tires wriggling.

"Find out what has to be done if a car was to lose control, causing the tires to come off unexpectedly," the voice prompted with a sense of urgency. She was puzzled. "How so?" she wondered. No one in her family, not even her relatives, had a car. Many questions flooded her mind.

So, she asked her friend who sat next to her in the moving, open van they were in, what he would do in such a situation. He quickly gave a quick, off-hand reply, "Whatever you do, never try to jump out of a moving car on the main road." His response was not just laced with maturity and wisdom. It was divinely inspired. As it turned out, there were other people around who also heard him when he said that.

Not long after that, a car whizzed past the race tracks. Apparently, the driver had been struggling with the brakes, trying his best to bring the car to a halt. But it would not respond. There was pandemonium, and everyone was thrown into a frenzy. The students panicked and ran for their lives as they held onto each other in fear of death. The driver did all he could to control the vehicle but to no avail. Suddenly, the tires came off, and everyone started screaming as the vehicle staggered on, lurching into the deep. Having lost its way, it halted by a small tree that stood right across the tracks.

It was at that precise moment that it dawned on her what had just happened. It was exactly what the Lord had earlier warned her about. The incident taught her a fundamental lesson - that God is always protecting us without us knowing. We call it luck, but it goes beyond that. And it's not luck either because, in a world of good and evil, there is no luck but pure rescue from evil.

As the sun kissed the earth goodbye and faded into the blackness of the night, Mwape took her favourite sleeping position and surrendered herself to the caress of the cool midnight breeze. She had barely slept for an hour when she had a dream. It was a replay of the accident in the valley. This time around, the details were somewhat gory, but she did her best to keep the memory of it all as she woke up.

In the dream, she saw a car crash heavily into a very big obstacle. And within seconds, there was a great conflagration, the flames furiously curling their way up into the open skies above. Blood was flowing everywhere. It came from the broken bones and torn veins of the victims of the ghastly accident. It was difficult to tell the number of those who survived or died. But there were serious casualties. The scene looked quiet except for the noisy wails and shrill cries of mothers and fathers who knew the pain of losing a child, children who saw first-hand the trauma of losing their guardian angels, and spouses who understood the dilemma of losing a lover. Those who managed to control their emotions were busy trying to rescue those who were hurt in the accident. Then she woke up. Thankfully, it was only a dream. In waking life, when the real accident happened, the disaster was averted, and everyone escaped unhurt. It was then it dawned on her that the horrific details of what she saw in the dream were what the Devil had planned for the accident in the valley. However, what was evident to everyone was that the small tree in the valley was actually an angel sent by God to avert the disaster.

Therefore, from Mwape's experience, it is clear to see that being saved from the accident in the valley was not just luck but an act of God, purely saving them from death and preserving them unto life. The bible says, "Fear not, for I am with you; Be not dismayed, for I am your God. I will strengthen you, Yes, I will help you, I will uphold you with My righteous right hand" Isaiah 41:10. It also says, "For God so loved the world that He gave His only begotten Son, that whoever believes in Him should not perish but have everlasting life" (John 3:16). Like salvation, Jesus dying on the cross and taking on our sins is not just a story about a good prophet but the Son of God who is pure in nature and without any blemish, coming down like a lamb to take away our sin. He traded His life for us, redeeming us from the debt that leads to death by dying for our sins.

Out of His abundant love, He frees us from Satan's abuse, misuse, captivity, enslavement and brings us into His everlasting life of rest to enjoy his kingdom on earth through love, peace, and joy in the Holy Ghost. "But God demonstrates His own love toward us, in that while we were still sinners, Christ died for us" (Romans 5:8).

You must understand that the intention of God for you is pure and true. God sees you no matter where you are or whatever situation you're in. Stop doubting that God sees and knows you, your needs, fears, expectations, desires, and deepest prayer points. Whatever you do, don't doubt God. Trust His timing and believe that even though He's four days late, He's still on time, and He'll show up just right when you need Him the most. The book of Ecclesiastes 3:1-8 teaches us the value and importance of respecting times and seasons.

"To everything, there is a season, and a time to every purpose under the heaven: And a time to be born, and a time to die; a time to plant, and a time to pluck up that which is planted; A time to kill, and a time to heal; a time to break down, and a time to build up; A time to weep, and a time to laugh; a time to mourn, and a time to dance; A time to cast away stones, and a time to gather stones together; a time to embrace, and a time to refrain from embracing; A time to get, and a time to lose; a time to keep, and a time to cast away; A time to rend, and a time to sew; a time to keep silence, and a time to speak; A time to love, and a time to hate; a time of war, and a time of peace."

God is orderly and knows just the appropriate time to do a thing. Remember, God had earlier shown Mwape that one of her children would die and that at a later time, her family would be struck with Covid-19. Well, seeing it in a vision doesn't mean it will or won't happen. Sometimes, it may come to pass. Sometimes, it may not. However, if you pray about it, you may overcome it. Yet, if the situation you find yourself aligns with God's will, plan, purpose, and the timing of your life, you may just have to learn to trust God. Let go and let God in.

A story is told of Hezekiah in the bible. He was diagnosed with a terminal sickness. According to the physicians who treated his case, he didn't have much time to live. God had already decided that he would never recover from his sickness. And to show the certainty of his tragic death, the Lord confirmed it by the word of His renowned servant, Isaiah. "In those days,

Hezekiah became ill and was at the point of death. The prophet Isaiah son of Amoz, went to him and said, 'This is what the Lord says: Put your house in order, because you are going to die; you will not recover" Isaiah 38:1.

What a declaration! Everyone would agree that when the Lord says a thing, there's a tone of finality that is usually attached to it. But some people are audacious in their demonstration of "crazy" faith. Hezekiah dared to confront God in the situation. He would not take no for an answer and chose to contradict God's promise and have good health and long life. So, he made a case with God, refusing to accept such a negative pronouncement over his life. In verse two, "Hezekiah turned his face to the wall and prayed to the Lord."

Such boldness can only come from a place of confidence in your relationship with God. Even the scriptures tell us to "go boldly before the throne of grace (Hebrews 4:16) and to bring forth our strong reasons whenever we pray to God" (Isaiah 41:21). This, Hezekiah understood, and that's why in verse three, he prayed, "'Remember, Lord, how I have walked before you faithfully and with wholehearted devotion have done what is good in your eyes.' And Hezekiah wept bitterly."

Hezekiah's story teaches believers how to pray effectively to achieve exceptional results. Why did he weep? It wasn't just because of the emotional weight of God's pronouncement of death over him. It was because he knew the word of God, which says, "The sacrifices of God are a broken spirit and a contrite heart. A contrite heart will the Lord not despise" (Psalm 51:17). He understood the place of being humble and vulnerable when you come to God in prayers.

See what happened in verse four of Isaiah 38. Immediately, the Lord heard Hezekiah's prayers, and He quickly interrupted Prophet Isaiah's journey back home. "'Go and tell Hezekiah, 'This is what the LORD, the God of your father David, says: I have heard your prayer and seen your tears; I will add fifteen years to your life. And I will deliver you and this city from the hand of the king of Assyria. I will defend this city. This is the Lord's sign to you that the LORD will do what he has promised. I will make the sun's shadow cast by the sun go back the ten steps it has gone down on the stairway of Ahaz." So the sunlight went backwards ten steps" Isaiah 38:5-8.

What a supernatural turnaround! From the above passage, you can see that in addition to longevity, God also gave other blessings to Hezekiah, which He sealed up with a promise. Anything is possible as long as it aligns with God's will for your life.

In the case of the young boy who died from cancer, the narrative is different. Prayers were made just like Hezekiah did. But unfortunately, he died. This does not mean that the Lord didn't honour the prayers made on the young boy's behalf or that he wasn't important to be reconsidered by God. It was only that God saw what others couldn't see and decided it was best to grant him eternal rest, and that's the reason God made arrangements to get him saved before his eventual passing.

It's tough to lose someone so dear to you. The pain is usually tormenting, and it isn't easy to heal. Worse still, tough to move on. Although, you may cry, pray, and fast for as long as you can. But if it's God's time and will, nothing can change it. In the instance of death, here's what you need to understand.

Death is being absent with you in body but present with God. So when you wonder why God didn't show up when anyone you love dies, it's because God has a different plan, and God desires for them to be in Heaven as long as you are a bornagain Christian. What if you learned more about where they were? Would it comfort you a little bit more?

Here's another story of Mwape's near-death experience.

When she was younger, she suffered from an illness that led to her death. To her, she didn't die. She simply fell asleep and started living again. It was like how real life feels in a dream. It's the same with death. However, maybe someday someone will prove that we experience some form of death to the flesh when we sleep and step into the spiritual realm - but that's another topic altogether.

So, in that moment of death, she found herself walking across a strange land, not like anywhere she's ever seen before in waking life. It was lush and evergreen. Everything came alive on that land as she walked on. She could hear people talking over the hill. It was another experience altogether that enchanted her. The thought of meeting them excited her, stirring an intense urge to walk up to them and start a conversation. As she made a move towards them, she heard her mother crying and calling out her name. As they say, the body can be dead, but the sense of hearing is the last to go. She wanted to stay longer in that place, but another thought hit her, "Let me see why Mom is crying, then I will return."

As she managed to gain consciousness, she had a lot of difficulties eating or drinking. Amid her struggle, the Lord gave her a scripture. It was Psalms 23:1-3a. It is a popular passage of the scripture, and the words are the exact ones they used to sing in Sunday School. It says, "The Lord is my shepherd; I shall not want. He makes me to lie down in green pastures; He leads me beside the still waters. He restores my soul." Due to her condition, she couldn't even sing the song as she didn't have the strength to do so. So, her mother sang it on her behalf as they both made their way to the hospital. After much medical help and by God's grace, she was restored to life and in perfect health. However, the only thing she lacked was strength which was due to her inability to eat.

The reality of death is that to a dying person, it was a joyful place to go to, but to the ones you're leaving behind, it is usually a sad moment. May the good Lord help you find peace in your grief. Although it takes time as you may have invested your love in these individuals, just like Mwape, who has also experienced the bitterness of losing someone, you may be comforted knowing you asked for help, and it came. But at the same time, you must take consolation in the fact that God saved our loved ones from their pain and struggles of life. I speak peace upon you in Jesus's name. Amen.

And sometimes, you're faced with more challenging situations that you begin to wonder if God is truly aware of your predicament or why He never showed up for you when you needed Him. Like Mwape, you may feel alone, especially when it's tough for you to get to the end of your rope successfully. Yet, there is something that she learned over the space of time which you, too, must understand. It is that sometimes God is busy helping and protecting us. When you think He is not there, He is actually there watching over you. But the problem is that sometimes we don't even notice it because we think we're just plain lucky and God is not involved in our rescue. That is a big misconception. It's never about luck. It's about God's grace and mercy.

Once upon a time in Israel, King Saul hated David and tried every means to destroy him. Aside from the fact that the king was regularly haunted by an evil spirit, he was also jealous of David. His jealousy drove him to do many unthinkable things in an attempt to kill him. Fortunately for David, he escaped being pinned to the wall by a javelin hurled at him by a furious king a few times. Some may attribute David's deliverance from such a furious onslaught as a product of skill, wit, or talent. But there was more. God knew everything that Saul had planned. So, whenever David ventured into the trap by chance, God was always awake and standing by to protect him each time. It was by the same token of God's grace and love for David that he was able to kill a giant (Goliath) with just five mere stones.

So, next time you manage to escape something tragic and painful, it is God who made it possible because He still loves and cares for you. And when you come to a point where you have tried your best with nothing else to do, it could be a sign that it's time you let God make the final decision over such matters. Sometimes it is best for our sanity and peace of mind to simply let go and let God.

Chapter Summary

We must stop making God insignificant by attributing our safety and deliverance to our luck.

It may seem like God is not there with you in a difficult situation and that He is far from you. But that is not true. Like the fourth person in the fire with Shadrach, Meshach, and Abednego, He knows when to show up so that He can confound your enemies. Do keep trusting Him.

Whenever God reveals that something bad is about to happen, it is usually a sign of victory for us. However, we must act promptly and obediently to avert whatever may happen.

God is always faithful and merciful to His children.

In the next chapter, you will learn...

The most important reason why women should not be underrated in ministry.

How you can use godly wisdom to handle oppressors who misrepresent the word of God.

Why it is important for you to do God's will irrespective of your gender and regardless of the oppression you face.

CHAPTER FOUR

The Oppression

Immediately she began to hear the voice of God more clearly and started following His lead. Mwape lost her popularity, and she no longer enjoyed the companionship of the people who were once close to her. Instead, she was oppressed on every front. Those who could either mentor her or support the work of God which she was doing were seen trying all they could to sabotage her teaching ministry, and it seemed it would be a difficult journey after all.

To some of her oppressors, the Lord personally visited in the night and told them that she was His servant. Following the revelation, one of the Leaders, during one of the services and in front of everyone, confessed that indeed Mwape was called by God. And right there on the altar, offered to mentor her. He was particularly very concerned for her and other youths in the church that whenever she or any of them missed a service, he prayed and fasted for them as the Lord led him.

To another, an angel also visited and asked them to repent and clear her reputation, which they were trying to destroy. When they refused, they went mad until they repented and confessed to Mwape all they had done to her. As soon as they had made their restitution, she prayed for their deliverance, and the illness left them. Unfortunately, others hadn't quite learned their lesson as they still kept on attacking her. But because it was more painful to see her oppressors suffer, Mwape repented on their behalf and asked the Lord to heal her and fill her heart with His love to enable her to overlook things and forgive the believers who constantly attacked her.

Nonetheless, Mwape was someone that enjoyed engaging in meaningful conversations with people. She's had theist heated discussions with at least 30 or more people against her, and she had usually found a way to win them over. But not always. There were several occasions where she'd been confronted by people who didn't agree with most of her teachings. And in such situations, she always found a way to explain the topics under discussion.

As Mwape progressed in her Christian journey, teaching, mentoring, and inspiring others to follow the Lord with all their hearts, it seemed so easy so far. But she was yet to scratch the surface of the ministry for which the Lord had called her. Her critics grew in their numbers; those who felt she was not qualified to teach, those who thought she lacked the experience, and those who believed that a priestly ministry is no place for females.

The more her critics went against her, the more determined than ever she became never to be a victim of oppression. She was not of the breed who would be silenced for the gospel of Christ. So, she remained dedicated to the call of God upon her life.

A familiar story in the bible comes to mind. It is about Elisha, who was Elijah's mentee and protegee. The time had come for Elijah to be taken away into heaven while Elisha stepped into his shoes as the prophet of Israel. However, there was a price to pay, and Elisha would have to prove that he was qualified to operate in that capacity as the new spiritual leader of the people.

As they both journeyed towards Bethel, the sons of the prophets stood by to discourage Elisha saying, "Knowest thou that the Lord will take away thy master from thy head today? And he replied simply, "Yea, I know it; hold ye your peace." The same thing happened at Jericho and Jordan. The sons of the prophets were also there to sow the seed of self-doubt and unbelief in Elisha. Unfortunately for them, he was not of that stock.

There was nothing anyone could do to deter him. He understood the gravity of what was at stake, and he was not ready to let such an uncommon opportunity slip from his grasp. His determination was greatly rewarded. He received a double portion of Elijah's power, making him perform his master's last miracle as his first. And this was only the beginning of the greatness he was to experience in his ministry.

It is not uncommon for people to attempt to kill your light, especially when doing exceptional things. The gender bias in ministry has become deep-rooted in Christianity as some women are often relegated to the background, and some men do all they can to ensure that their place is recognized. Some men give all forms of excuses and reasons, including using illustrations from the bible to buttress their point. Yet, some women, too, are called by God just as men.

Although this suppression sometimes was not direct, she felt it even for other women. She could not watch them being silenced when it is glaring how God has worked with women throughout the scriptures. For example, Rebeccah, Isaac's wife, whom God shared the future of the children (Jacob and Esau) with, Esther, whom God entrusted to deliver the Jews when they needed her help, Deborah, who was a Judge and a prophetess over Israel, Mary, the mother of Jesus, etc.

With this understanding and conviction, she went back to God in prayers and asked how she was supposed to win souls when Apostle Paul wrote something that works against the women. Then the Holy Spirit spoke very clearly to her and taught her the word of God. All along, she had thought that she always had to see herself as a "son" meaning seeing yourself as a Daughter was wrong, as though God only wanted male children, but the Holy spirit made her realise sonship was to do with Maturity in faith not gender And immediately after her encounter with the Holy Spirit, her eyes were opened to the fact that she is also special as a woman in the eyes of God.

Again, the Holy Spirit took her to the book of Genesis 3:1-6, 8-13 and expounded the word of God more profoundly. It says,"

Then the serpent said to the woman, 'You will not surely die. For God knows that on the day you eat of it your eyes will be opened, and you will be like God, knowing good and evil.' So when the woman saw that the tree was good for food, that it was pleasant to the eyes, and a tree desirable to make one wise, she took of its fruit and ate.

She also gave it to her husband with her, and he ate it. And they heard the sound of the Lord God walking in the garden in the cool of the day, and Adam and his wife hid themselves from the presence of the Lord God among the trees of the garden. Then the Lord God called to Adam and said to him, 'Where are you?' So he said, 'I heard your voice in the garden, and I was afraid because I was naked; and I hid myself.'

Genesis 3:15

And He said, 'Who told you that you were naked? Have you eaten from the tree of which I commanded you that you should not eat?' Then the man said, 'The woman whom You gave to be with me, she gave me of the tree, and I ate.' And the Lord God said to the woman, 'What is this you have done?' The woman said, 'The serpent deceived me, and I ate.'

"And I will put enmity between thee and the woman, and between thy seed and her seed (children of God and Satan's);

it/He/Jesus shall bruise thy/Your head, and thou shalt bruise his heel (under his feet position). ((to do With Jesus having Authority over the Devil and all his demonic children)

Unto the woman he said, I will greatly multiply thy sorrow and thy conception; in sorrow/labour pains thou shalt bring forth children, and thy desire shall be to thy/your husband, and he shall rule over thee. (that's it, that's all he did to Eve, he did not call her names, he did not beat her, oppress her, nor guilt shame her)

And unto Adam, he said, "Because thou hast hearkened unto the voice of thy wife, and hast eaten of the tree, of which I commanded thee, saying, 'Thou shalt not eat of it,' cursed is the ground for thy sake.' (Basically, I've cursed someone else on your behalf because God can't curse what he has blessed) In sorrow/work shalt thou eat of it all the days of thy life; Thorns also and thistles shall it bring forth to thee, and thou shalt eat the herb of the field; In the sweat of thy face shalt thou/you eat bread, till thou return unto the ground; for out of it wast thou taken: for dust thou art, and unto dust shalt thou return.

(Adam was punished with food - as they say, the secret to a man's heart is food. So again, a reminder to say every time you are eating something, remember that day.) "Another rainbow moment".

From these scriptures, she began to notice God's reaction to Adam and Eve. Yes, they died spiritually, but something else happened to them. The Lord revealed Adam's life before the fall, whereby he did not have to worry about food or shoes as the Garden in Eden had no thorns nor thistles, and he did not sweat to get what he wanted. Yet we see that after the fall, God did not curse Adam. Instead, he cursed the ground and told Adam he would have to work for his food and sweat for things in life. We see Adam being demoted from king to slave and from a rich man in charge to a poor man. As for Eve, her punishment was to desire her husband, with him ruling over her. And that every time she and many women after that were having a child, we would be reminded of her in birth pains.

But here is how God dealt with women. He first assured her, saying there is hope, which is the part most people don't see. Before telling Eve that every time she had a baby, she would be reminded of that day, like he told Noah that the rainbow is a sign of the covenant that he would not destroy the earth with rain again, he ASSURED EVE.

In Genesis 3:15, he said: "And I will put enmity between thee and the woman,(telling Satan), and between thy seed and her seed; it shall bruise thy head, and thou shalt bruise his heel." (Heel means you are under his feet.) Wow!

In short, God was saying, 'Satan, you thought you were clever bringing in sin through a woman.' He then provided a way out for them through another woman. If God regretted women, he would not have involved them in the 2nd Adam Jesus, but since it began with a woman, God ended it with a woman: Mary. Thus, Eve is redeemed. If we refuse to accept Eve's redemption, we refuse to accept the church's redemption as we are all Eve, both men and women.

Lastly, God did not cut his ties with Adam and Eve. If anything, after they had children, we hear about him fellowshipping with Eve's children, Cain and Abel. So ask yourselves, why are you condemning what God has not condemned?

From these scriptures, she also discovered that Apostle Paul said women should not be teachers and should learn in silence. And if they had any questions, they ought to ask their husbands at home. Even at that, she realized there was something wrong with these statements and that the context in which people were using them was wrong.

Now Paul was a man of great influence and a father of the gentile church, which we are all a part of. Apostle Paul dealt with issues of life, including marriage, and from his text, you can tell he was almost like a marriage counsellor because he is one of the leaders known to focus on the subject of marriage in the New Testament more than others. However, his teachings are somewhat difficult to understand. You will need the insight of the Holy Spirit or the guidance of unbiased, devoted spiritual leaders and mentors to help you gain clarity.

From the book of Genesis, Mwape realized that Eve represents the Church and Adam, Christ. And, as we know, only Adam is not from a woman, but every other man came through or from a woman.

It means men that are born from women are part of that church that is being cleansed. With that in mind, let's realize that both men and women can be deceived. There are only two Adams; through the first Adam, we all died according to the word of God, and through the 2nd Adam, Jesus, we are made alive.

We see the example of Peter in Matthew 16:23. He had tried to stop our Lord Jesus from going into Jerusalem, thinking it was his original idea. Unknown to him, it was the Devil using him as his mouthpiece. And when Jesus realized what was happening, he quickly rebuked him, saying, "Get thee behind me, Satan!" Though Peter was being mentored by Jesus and walked with Him, he was not like Adam just by being a man.

Another instance is in the story of Jesus and the gentile woman who needed healing. He had told her that bread (meaning healing) was for the children (the Jews) and not dogs (gentiles). The phrase "dogs" as being used in the scriptures is used to describe everyone not of the Jewish race. But John made a shocking revelation in John 1:11-12, which says, "He came to his own, and his own received him not, but as many (gentiles included) as received him, to them gave he the power to become the sons (Christ likes) of God, even to them that believed on his name."

It also says in Galatians 3:28 that "There is neither Jew nor Greek, there is neither bond nor free, there is neither male nor female: for ye are all one in Christ Jesus."

If Paul's statement were to be considered literally, then we would have a society of holy men and sinful women. But instead, what we see is children of God, Jews, and gentiles. Hence, the reason the church is referred to as the bride of Christ as seen in the above scriptures. In 1 Corinthians 11:11-12, Paul says again, "Nevertheless neither is the man without the woman, neither the woman without the man, in the Lord. For as the woman is of the man, even so is the man also by the woman; but all things of God."

So, the story of Adam and Eve was not necessarily about a woman's weakness but mankind and their response when they go wrong, which is to blame others and not take responsibility that can lead to repentance.

It's a story of a man that loved his wife so much that he decided to fall with her. If Adam was not deceived, it means he knew what he was doing. Our Lord Jesus did the same too. Only that He did not sin with his bride, the church (both males and females) but took the blame on her behalf, a punishment that led to his death, and when he came back to life after defeating death and Satan, He was able to present His bride again before God blameless.

Ask yourself, if every woman had to learn in silence and ask for scriptural understanding from their husbands, wouldn't that be a great assumption that all women are married and that they are married to bible scholars? And if that was the case, why did Paul say in other scriptures that an unbelieving husband is sanctified through his believing wife? It means Paul was fully aware that not all believing women married bible scholars or born-again husbands.

So, what's the right context? In marriage, men are the image of God, looking at it from their perspective being called the father since God is also called Father. From first-hand experience, it's hard to think of God never leaving or forsaking you, especially when your earthly father did. This is also the reason why Mwape struggled to relate with God as Father, considering her experience. But when she eventually did, it was the greatest deliverance from pain, unforgiveness, bitterness, etc. So, giving it to the men, they actually play a big role in marriage and in a child's life.

God demands that women should submit to their own husbands. However, women respond to love, care, affection, and attention when received. When you love a woman like she should be loved, your ideas, dreams, and aspirations will be hers, and she will do her best to help you become fulfilled. As Miles Monroe said, women multiply whatever a man gives them. When you give them negativity, they multiply it and give you hell, but if you give them love, they multiply it and give you a baby. So, men and women are meant to complement each other. This is the perfect image God was referring to in the book of Genesis.

Women generally multitask. This is a high-demand skill in ministry. As men are busy with other ministerial assignments, women also help out whichever way they can to enable the work of God to progress rapidly. Also, the woman or wife needs the husband to help her do one thing at a time and not start too many things and finish none. Men also need support in terms of contributing ideas, suggestions, resources, etc. from the women especially when he has other activities at hand.

After expounding the scriptures to them, they realized they were reading the scriptures out of context. Mwape also made them understand that Delilah and Jezebel were not Jews, and so have no comparison to any Christian girl, but that even men can be Delilahs after a downfall of a Christian girl. And men can go against other ministers too. This, we have seen in social media that the "Jezebelic" spirit is a spirit that knows no gender.

And with that, Mwape was finally able to get the attention of the men. But it was because she had a solid grasp of the scriptures and used it as a weapon against her oppressors whenever the occasion called for it. If you must overcome temptation or be victorious over your oppressors, you must know what the scriptures say in certain situations and learn how to use them appropriately.

Chapter Summary

The most important thing in life is knowing how to stay focused in the face of strong opposition and criticism.

A Church is like a Rehabilitation centre- everyone is working on something, no one is perfect. With that in mind, focus on the cross and what the Lord is doing in you and you will have no time to see what others are doing.

Regardless of your gender, God can still use you to do His will. Always go back to God whenever you're faced with stiff opposition.

Remember the Bible says in Joel 2vs 28, "Your sons and daughters shall prophesy." Ladies be encouraged, God saw that men needed a helper and called 999 and a woman turned up. You are also just as important and needed in God's kingdom business!

Knowing what the word of God says can be a lifesaver most times.

Know when not to defend yourself in words, let your lifestyle speak for you.

In the next chapter, you will learn...

The value of prayer in any situation you find yourself in.

Why fear is dangerous and why you must overcome it.

The secret to overcoming fear - looking unto Jesus. He, who saves us from our most dreaded situations.

CHAPTER FIVE

The Coronavirus Siege

In 2019, the world was ravaged by the Covid-19 pandemic. Everyone was scared, but Mwape was not of that breed. Her faith in God had soared. Unlike others, she was quick to realize that fear caused panic. And those who succumbed to the power of fear were worst hit by the pandemic. And her family was not spared in the siege, so she resorted to prayers.

*As she prayed, she saw a mara Vision, in this vision she saw an army of angels, so numerous that she could not count them, as she was drawn closer, she saw a fountain of waters, and she asked the Lord for cleansing and to be filled up with the flood of the Living waters the Holy Spirit, she was cleansed and filled up. Later she saw the LORD seating on a chair, and he draw her closer to himself and began to share his assignment to her and revealed what was going on around the world.

*Now, the mara vision, it's the one you see that affects your body and your environment, so the people around you can also feel the tangible presence of God. The experience was so great that when her husband touched her, the illness left his body instantly, much like the woman healed of cancer. She also went on to pray for everyone in the house, and the following day they all looked better.

However, barely two days later, just when she thought it was over, Mwape was struggling to breathe. Initially, she only had migraines, but the struggle for breath only grew stronger and stronger. She went before God on her knees, but her voice could not come out as she panicked as though she would die of Covid-19. At that moment, she called her trusted godly parents and friends to stand for her, but everyone was asleep. So, she asked her husband to pray for her, and they both went to sleep.

Between life and death, she still held onto God and His plan for her life. The thought of leaving her baby and her 2-year-old son, a husband that needs her help to stand strong as a family, and siblings, just made the certainty of death real. As she laid down in bed, she started to profess and remind the Lord what He had revealed to her. The good and bad landmarks she'd gone through. So she said to the Lord, "Father, you said I had to go through this experience for the many people out there, and I refuse to die because you told me you would quicken the days to help me and that you could not stop it because what you have said has to happen because you are the God of Truth. Now, me dying would go against your name as you have shown me things that have not come to pass yet."

Although Mwape had prayed, there was still a part of her that felt unsure. She panicked like Peter, who lost his confidence when his feet touched the sea, and he walked on it. But fortunately for him, the Lord Jesus was standing by to help him. In this story, the most important thing to note was the assurance that the Lord gave Peter even though he felt like his end had come.

In Matthew 14:25-33, "Shortly before dawn, Jesus went out to them, walking on the lake. When the disciples saw him walking on the lake, they were terrified. 'It's a ghost," they said, and cried out in fear. But Jesus immediately said to them: 'Take courage! It is I. Don't be afraid.' 'Lord, if it's you,' Peter replied, 'tell me to come to you on the water.' 'Come,' he said. Then Peter got down out of the boat, walked on the water, and came towards Jesus. But when he saw the wind, he was afraid and, beginning to sink, cried out, 'Lord, save me!' Immediately Jesus reached out his hand and caught him. 'You of little faith,' he said, 'why did you doubt?' And when they climbed into the boat, the wind died down. Then those who were in the boat worshipped him, saying, 'Truly you are the Son of God.'"

Initially, Peter was very courageous. He believed that as long as the Lord Jesus gave him permission to walk on water, he would be safe, and no harm would come to him. And that was exactly what happened. Not for long, though, because as Peter managed to take the first few steps across the water, he became scared, lost faith in himself, and as a result, began to sink. The problem began when Peter lost his focus, paying attention to the wind, waves, and currents that swept across the sea instead of looking at Jesus, who had called him in the first place.

Peter didn't realize that the experience was meant to test his faith and resolve in the Lord. When Jesus gave him that assignment, He wanted to test the depth of his faith and how much trust and confidence he reposed in the Word of the Lord.

Sometimes, we are like Peter, feeling too confident simply because the Lord had called us. The excitement pushes us to attempt what the Lord has given us to do. But when push comes to shove, and the challenges seem more than we can bear, selfdoubt arises, and we start to fall apart. There is a fundamental lesson to learn from Peter's story: when the Lord gives you his Word, trust Him enough to do just as He has said without giving room to the enemy to make you question your healing, breakthrough, success, or whatever He has promised you.

Even though the rest of Mwape's family had started experiencing divine healing from the Coronavirus, she started to have doubts when her situation grew worse without any sign of getting better. As soon as she opened a window of doubt, fear set in immediately, and she started to focus on the possibility of dying instead of the Word of the Lord.

That is exactly what fear does. It makes you imagine the worst. It paints a gloomy picture of your situation and makes it believable, that in the face of difficult situations - you can "Forget Everything And Run." This is due to ignorance and the fact that fear itself is "False Evidence Appearing Real." But the people who overcome fear are those with incredible faith and courage even in the midst of dire circumstances. This is how they overcome fear: focus on Jesus the AUTHOR and FINISHER OF OUR FAITH.

In Matthew 8: 23-26, there is another story of fear. The disciples were confronted by nature while voyaging on the sea. When the storm came, they were very frightened even though this time, the Lord was with them in the boat. "Now, when He got into a boat, His disciples followed Him. And suddenly, a great tempest arose on the sea so that the boat was covered with the waves. But He was asleep. Then His disciples came to Him and awoke Him, saying, 'Lord, save us! We are perishing!' But He said to them, 'Why are you fearful, O you of little faith?' Then He arose and rebuked the winds and the sea, and there was a great calm."

From this story, it is clear that it goes beyond just knowing that Jesus is always near you to have faith. Knowledge is not enough. It doesn't matter how much you know the Lord. The disciples were even closer to Him. The Lord has to live in you for your faith to have full power. This is why the bible says, "Greater is he that is in us than he that is in the world…" Elisha bore witness to this truth when he told his servant, "Be not afraid. For they that are with us are greater than they that are with them." To reach this height of faith, you must have a deep personal relationship with the Lord. and "let the word of God dwell in you richly." Suffice to say, you must live the Word. Live boldly and without fear.

In a moment of panic, we tend to forget all that God is capable of and succumb to the pressures of Satan, and this is what happens when we not only let our guards down but when we lose focus and allow our present circumstances to decide our fate. We need to learn from our Lord Jesus and see how he dealt with the devil when he tried to confuse Him and introduce doubt.

Let's see what happened in Matthew 4:1-11, "Then Jesus was led up by the Spirit into the wilderness to be tempted by the devil. And when He had fasted forty days and forty nights, afterwards He was hungry. Now when the tempter came to Him, he said, 'If You are the Son of God, command that these stones become bread.' But He answered and said, 'It is written, 'Man shall not live by bread alone, but by every word that proceeds from the mouth of God.' Then the devil took Him up into the holy city, set Him on the pinnacle of the temple, and said to Him, 'If You are the Son of God, throw Yourself down. For it is written: 'He shall give His angels charge over you,' and, 'In their hands they shall bear you up, Lest you dash your foot against a stone.' Jesus said to him, 'It is written again, 'You shall not tempt the Lord your God.' Again, the devil took Him up on an exceedingly high mountain, and showed Him all the kingdoms of the world and their glory. And he said to Him, 'All these things I will give You if You will fall down and worship me.' Then Jesus said to him, 'Away with you, Satan! For it is written, 'You shall worship the Lord your God, and Him only you shall serve.' Then the devil left Him, and behold, angels came and ministered to Him."

From the above scriptures, we learn that not only did Jesus not entertain doubt, but he also rebuked every Word with scriptures, and the devil did flee from him. God's desire is for you to live a life without fear because fear weakens our view of God and empowers the devil. There are a plethora of fearful people in the bible who went on to do great things because they took every Word of God seriously and obeyed in totality.

Let's see the example of Joshua in Joshua 1:1-3, 5-7, 9, "After the death of Moses the servant of the Lord, it came to pass that the Lord spoke to Joshua the son of Nun, Moses' assistant, saying: 'Moses My servant is dead. Now, therefore, arise, go over this Jordan, you and all these people, to the land which I am giving to them - the children of Israel. Every place that the sole of your foot will tread upon I have given you, as I said to Moses. No man shall be able to stand before you all the days of your life; as I was with Moses, so I will be with you. I will not leave you nor forsake you. Be strong and of good courage, for to these people you shall divide as an inheritance the land which I swore to their fathers to give them. Only be strong and very courageous, that you may observe to do according to all the law which Moses My servant commanded you; do not turn from it to the right hand or to the left, that you may prosper wherever you go. Have I not commanded you? Be strong and of good courage; do not be afraid, nor be dismayed, for the Lord your God is with you wherever you go.'"

Doesn't this sound like a love letter from a Father to a son? Obviously, the voice of God encouraging him not to be afraid but to be strong and of good courage was enough assurance that He would always be with him as He was with Moses, his mentor. In the same vein, we should always hold on to whatever the Lord tells us and, beyond that, believe Him wholeheartedly and act obediently at all times.

Chapter Summary

To attempt great things in life, courage is a vital quality. No matter how dark it may seem, there is always light at the end of the tunnel.

Hold on to God's word, no matter how long it takes. Habakuk 2:3 says, "For the vision is yet for an appointed time, but at the end it shall speak, and not lie: though it tarry, wait for it; because it will surely come, it will not tarry."

In whatever situation you find yourself, never let fear decide your fate.

Learn to trust God. It may seem like a difficult thing to do, especially in the most challenging circumstances.

In the next chapter, you will learn...

All things are possible with God.

If there is a man to pray, there is a God to listen.

The importance of healthy, natural diets in our physical and spiritual wellbeing.

CHAPTER SIX

Prophetic Healing

Mum woke up one fine morning, eager to go to work as usual. She was dressed in her favourite clothes, looking ravishingly beautiful as she took one final gaze at the mirror that stood a few steps away from her. She blushed as the mirror revealed how gorgeous she looked that morning. And with a smile that warmed the entire house, she greeted everyone and bade them goodbye. And with that, she drove off to work.

If there was one thing she was passionate about, it was seeing people leading happy, healthy lives. For this reason, she dedicated her life to the medical profession to fulfil that dream of hers. She had never had a busier time than in 2019 when the Coronavirus pandemic became a global catastrophe. And as a frontline worker, her job demanded a lot from her and exposed her to some risks.

She arrived at the hospital early, took the vaccine that day, and later went to her workplace at a residential home. She began her routine tasks as scheduled.

Work that day was busy, as she had to cover for a work colleague. The situation was overwhelming, and it put everyone on duty under intense pressure. In the heat of these activities, one of the health workers found out they were infected. She had contracted the virus. To control the extent of the damage done, they had to trace those she'd been in contact with. Mom was among them, and unfortunately, she tested positive for the virus. Upon realizing how badly the virus hit her, she quickly isolated herself from the rest of the family.

Not long before that day, Mwape had a dream of a death spirit coming after a woman. She quickly told her mentor, Apostle Joshua Marlon, about it. He was someone who always prayed for her family. And he said to her "Start praying in tongues!"

Mom's symptoms were typical of the Coronavirus - difficulty breathing, loss of taste and smell, etc. She was also unable to walk a long distance or speak without struggling to breathe. This situation forced Mwape to wake up as early as 4- 5 am, ensuring everyone was alive and well. During one of her early morning routines, she received inspiration from the Holy Spirit to make a home remedy for the treatment of Covid-19. It was a mixture of ginger, lemon, garlic, onion, and orange. She administered the remedy to every member of her family. However, Mom didn't take it. Instead, she took a little bit of ginger, lemon, and hot water.

Shortly after, Mwape's husband and children miraculously began to recover, but Mom was still struggling to breathe. And that bothered Mwape a great deal, causing her faith to wane, seeing her mother wasn't getting any better. The more she panicked, the more she, too, struggled to breathe. And it was in that moment that a deep sleep fell upon her, and the Lord showed her that Mom was going to be well. As soon as Mwape woke from her sleep, she declared the word of the Lord, which she shared with everyone.

And with that encouragement from the Lord, her faith soared again. She believed God for her Mom's healing and used that same faith to believe in everyone's healing, and as it turned out, her entire family was made whole. This experience reminds me of what Jesus meant when He said He only does what He sees His Father do... "Then answered Jesus and said unto them, 'Verily, verily, I say unto you, the Son can do nothing of himself, but what he seeth the Father do: for what things so ever he doeth, these also doeth the Son likewise'" John 5:19 (KJV).

When she saw someone's healing in a vision, her faith was strong enough to bring the same to her family members too. It was a prophetic moment. Before now, she thought that to be a prophet, you had to have your own power. But now, it was clear that all power in heaven and on earth belongs to Jesus Christ, our Lord. "Behold, I give unto you power to tread on serpents and scorpions, and over all the power of the enemy: and nothing shall by any means hurt you" Luke 10:19 (KJV).

Soon after her whole family was healed, Mom's feet started to swell up, and her blood clot. So, she started looking for aspirin to thin the blood. But unfortunately, they were selfisolating, so it was a bit difficult to get any. At that point, the Holy Spirit prompted Mwape to look online to find out which home remedy had aspirin in them, where the home remedy that acted as aspirin was. It was the same remedy she'd been giving others but with turmeric. Added to the solution administered was a dose of turmeric, ginger, garlic, onion, lemon, and orange to ease the taste. The result? Not only was blood-thinning achieved, but she was able to walk and breathe normally. Suffice to say that her whole system was back to normal, and she went back to work two days later. Praise the Lord!

We can only live miraculously through Christ. He is indeed the author and finisher of our faith. He is our All in All, the Alpha and Omega, the Beginning of all things and the End. Indeed, all things hold together in Him. "For in Him, we live, move and have our being." HE IS THE GREAT I AM, OUR

ROCK OF AGES, OUR ALL-SUFFICIENT GOD! AND HIS NAME IS JESUS, THE MOST HIGH GOD!

Now someone may ask, "How is it possible that home remedies and faith in the supernatural power of God were able to treat the Coronavirus successfully?" To answer simply, here's the story of the young girl Jesus raised from the dead in Mark 5:41-43, "And he took the Damsel by the hand, and said unto her, Talitha cumi; which is, being interpreted, Damsel, I say unto thee, arise. And straightway the Damsel arose, and walked; for she was of the age of twelve years. And they were astonished with a great astonishment. And he charged them straight that no man should know it; and commanded that something should be given her to eat."

From the above passage, two things are of significance to note. First, we notice the supernatural display of the miracleworking power of God not just over sickness or a terminal disease but over death itself. Therefore, if the Lord could prevail over death, which is the end of all things, including life on earth, then the Coronavirus is definitely no match for the power God. Secondly, the Lord commanded the people to feed Damsel. The Lord recognized the importance of a healthy meal in staying alive. Of course, since she had just been resurrected, she definitely needed strength, and the only way to regain it was by giving her something to eat, which the Lord had already commanded.

So we learn that as much as God heals us or can raise us from the dead, the body still needs to be looked after the natural way. Look at the story of Elijah, the prophet of God that was fed by angels. The bible records the only time when God fed humanity with angel's food that fell from heaven when Moses and the Israelites were in the wilderness.

Even Jesus was hungry when He was in the wilderness. The bible records that when the enemy tempted Him to turn a stone into bread, He did not yield, and neither was He seen hungry again. Later, we saw Jesus looking for fruit on a fig tree, but it had no fruits. Jesus felt disappointed because the tree was not fulfilling its purpose. But that's not the catch. Even though Jesus had the power to make the tree come alive and bear fruits, He still didn't. This shows that He obeyed the mortal way of things, living more like a man than God.

There are endless possibilities with God because He is unlimited in power, might, and wisdom. But the world, through its physical, societal, and technological advancements, has somehow managed to blind us to that truth, forcing us to be dependent on human-made healthcare systems, governmental policies, systems, and structures only, while disregarding the existence of God's sovereign power. And that is why the world acts delusional in serious situations. Until we acknowledge that God reigns in the affairs of men, humanity will always be groping in obscurity, thinking that we can solve our problems on our own. There is no better time than now to jettison our oldfashioned beliefs in superficial innovations and discoveries, our erroneous mindsets, to experience the Spirit of God dwelling among men.

Chapter Summary

Wherever death is, the spirit of death is present. Wherever sickness is, the spirit of infirmity is found. In the same vein, when there is life, God is equally present. With that in mind, every Christian should first and foremost deal with the strong man through prayer in these circumstances.

The truth is that in these last days, there is a dimension of God you cannot experience until you come to the fullness of the maker of heaven and earth, the One who has the infinite wisdom that transcends human wisdom, ingenuity, scientific and medical innovations.

A popular maxim says, "health is wealth." Sometimes, we overlook natural remedies that could be potential health solutions because we underestimate their benefits.

The importance of eating healthy cannot be overemphasized as it also impacts your body, soul, and spirit.

It is important to trust God in everything, even in health, because, as they say, although the doctors may do their best to cure you, it is God that heals.

Always learn to listen to the "still small voice." Obey the Lord in everything, even if it doesn't seem humanly logical.

In the next chapter, you will learn...

Why depending on God is necessary for living a well-defined life that counts for the future.

The one thing everyone must focus on as they live their regular, everyday lives.

That with all certainty, the coming of the Lord is nearer than we once thought.

CHAPTER SEVEN

The Future

Over the months and years, Mwape enjoyed a deep, wellconnected relationship with the Lord. On many occasions, she'd had a vision where she'd see events of the future unfolding to her. Although her future visions were not in any particular order, it is important to share them with the rest of the world as there are salient messages that everyone should know.

It was just a few hours after her midnight prayers. As soon as she closed her eyes, she drifted into a deep sleep as fast as possible. Then one of her visions came again. It was about the rapture. She saw young street boys, dangerous-looking, chasing after her. As she ran, she met a Pastor whom she asked to pray for her as she was fast losing strength. When she did, she felt better. Shortly after that episode, she found herself with a group of other people riding in a car. As they sped on, she saw a thick cloud of darkness suddenly hovering around. As soon as it happened, she saw evil displayed on TV screens, especially in the form of music. At that moment, she found herself with other Christian women hiding in a see-through, glass-like tub, and they could see each other. It was a time of the antichrist mark. Later someone found them and marked the see-through glass cover with a red cross. For a moment, it felt like she was made unclean.

Then Mwape heard a voice that spoke clearly to her, "What's in your hand?" She replied, "It's a cross!" It was one of the Catholic crosses that usually glow green. Just then, the voice spoke again, this time louder than the first, "The power of the cross!" Immediately, the cross shone so bright it melted off the other cross, and the Light of God came upon them, and with the boldness of one backed up by an unseen supernatural presence, they came out clothed in light to be seen, and the people that were sent to attack them ran away. Then she heard someone echoing through the loudspeakers tactfully staged in the four corners of the auditorium. The voice had a familiar ring to it. As she listened closely, it turned out to be the voice of Pastor Benny Hinn praying in tongues. As he prayed in tongues, the heavens opened wider, and a window appeared in heaven with light escaping through it. Angels appeared around the door looking like doves from afar and were busy singing "Hosanna, Hosanna," so beautifully like rivers flowing so smoothly.

Soon after that, a sign appeared, and everyone knew that the Lord was coming. In that precise moment, everyone just knew things without words being exchanged. And immediately, everyone started praying for the salvation of their loved ones. Mwape knew that once the people saw the Lord, they would forget their present sorrows. And with that, she persisted in praying that they escape death and become saved so that they may be granted eternal life with Christ in Heaven.

Just then, the heavens opened with clouds coming down like a stairway. And, just as the book of revelation explained that He took all our worries and sorrows away, they all began to experience divine joy and peace in the presence of the Lord. Upon seeing Him and realizing that there was no one else behind Him, Mwape screamed loudly, "Jesus is Lord! Jesus is

Lord!!" And the rest of the conversations they had were without words.

Then something mysterious happened. It was as though she was split in two, her flesh on one part, her spirit on the other. Now, her body (flesh) was watching her spirit in fellowship with Jesus. Suffice to say, she was watching herself. While her body was praying in tongues, her heart was having a conversation with the Lord. They talked about what she had to do next, which apparently, was to get baptized in water, following which the ability to speak in tongues will come later when she comes to her natural, mortal state. She did that and asked her pastors to baptize her to receive the baptism of fire.

As soon as she woke from the dream, she realized that her natural body was shaking and cold at the same time. The episode reminded her of what happened to Daniel in the scriptures when he saw an angel and his body could not take it. After this revelation of the imminent return of the Lord, God began to open her eyes to see more things concerning the future, not just about herself or her family and friends, but about the whole world.

This time she saw herself in Africa. When she heard a tramped sound, she knew it was time to leave the earth and quickly repented. But before she could warn anyone to prepare for it, she disappeared and found herself on a moving train, with everyone raptured, the train with no doors. It was open, and anyone that got on it who was full of sin, was spat out of the moving train - like someone that had attended a wedding banquet in dirty clothes in Matthew 22:1-14 (since dirty clothes symbolize unforgiveness and many other unrepented sins).

Then she later found herself in a garden, with people that seemed to be in rehabilitation. She remembered you could not mention alcohol because a former alcoholic would become weak to it. This was a place where people that had just accepted

Jesus were groomed. They were being turned into sonship in the image and likeness of God. There was an angel present too. It reminded her of the bible verse that talks about Jesus preaching to the spirits, Peter 3:19.

Rapture

She saw another vision this was over 10yrs ago, that as people waited for rapture temptations came in all forms. She saw that to her it came in a form of unforgiveness, it seemed like the devil wanted to keep them from rupturing by all means, but mwape saw herself saying its not worth it, and repented and made up with her friend, around the time there were great evangelical works by youth and leaders too.

Then a sign appeared in the heaven and mwape new it was time, in the vision she saw herself being taken up, and she said to the ones that remained that it is happening accordingly... as they ascended up chariots picket them up and that was it

Quantum Computers

Once again, Mwape had another revelation. This time, it was about technology - quantum computers, to be precise. In her dream, she saw highly sophisticated technology entering marketplaces throughout the world in large numbers and someone asking her if they had figured out the quantum calculations. She saw the numbers "010101001." Immediately, she thought it didn't make sense and wondered whether it meant 10 x 100, but, no matter the calculations, they led in a circle. After that, she saw a silver-looking, oval-shaped molecule floating.

Then somewhere in the middle, a circle opened up, and an image that looked like a galaxy appeared inside. This technology was built to see through things, even planets, grounds, etc., so she'd heard. As she moved within the city, still in the dream, she saw that things had changed drastically. She saw advanced life, something akin to the sci-fi movies we've seen on the big screens. For a moment, Mwape felt like she was backwards to that life and system.

Then she saw one of her friends saying, "The vaccine is no longer compulsory. Dubai has found a cure. People are getting healed, and England has stopped forcing everyone to take the vaccines as it will be treated as just any other flu. Now, during her 'A' levels, she failed all her science subjects and, as a result, decided to drop them to go for other subjects. Technically speaking, before this dream, she had no idea what the word "quantum" meant, nor does she know what it is even now. She only knew about it from the dream and decided to search out what it was all about on Google. She woke up with a certainty that if the quantum computer is being worked on in waking life, it shall be achieved and that the cure for Covid-19 will soon be available.

The Vision of the Nephilims

While she slept one particular evening, she had yet another vision. She saw Nephilims living among men. They could take up bodies of men to look like us, normal individuals. And they caused trouble endlessly. They sometimes sprayed a substance on people, which caused them to lose their memory and so that they could more easily live among them. And if someone tried to fight back, they would return to their normal size, form, and ways. So, no one could defeat them. And still, they lived among us as our neighbours.

Soon after that, she had another dream. This time, she saw that a time of hardship was coming. She saw nations struggling for money but still kept on building luxurious houses, and even Africa looked good too. As everything was starting to take form, something tragic happened. It was so sudden no one saw it coming. It was like a global disaster, one in which many people would be led into captivity. But before that, people were busy looking for a prophet, or a man being used by God at that time, for salvation but could not find any. They were either silent, hiding, or it was difficult to decipher who the real prophet of God was. Thus, people grew more confused about who to run to for their deliverance.

The dream entered another scene with chaos and violence everywhere. And in those days, decent people started living like rascals and street urchins. At one point, people got abducted and were used as instruments of violence. But they fought their way to freedom eventually.

The Vision About Africa and Asia

In this particular dream, she saw that the Japanese, Koreans, and Chinese were hiring Africans, particularly Zambians, who knew how to communicate in their languages fluently. Also, Zambian companies were not hiring young people, especially fresh graduates. They saw them as immature and unable to handle complex situations, which the older folks handled casually.

As soon as that scene passed, Mwape saw a Korean flag flying on African streets. Many Asians lived among Africans and did business with them. They seemed too serious, and no one could understand their language. Only those who managed to understand what they were saying benefited from what they had to offer. Luckily, some people offered to teach these Asian languages. One easy way to befriend the Asians and enjoy their products and services was to smile often at the locals, learn how to speak their language, and find a middle-ground communication pathway. That way, even African businesses could thrive too.

A Time of Chaos

In this vision, people were killing and were being killed. She saw secret forces parading the entire city. They wore normal clothes, and no one dared to look at their faces. Anyone who saw them or realized who they were and was killed immediately. They were called the "212."

There were also black people fighting one another. This was not a regular fight. It is a fight to the death.

She later saw that some people had broken into the country, refugees and they were trying to fish them out. She also saw two young Chinese people who came to verify if Mwape was from the UK. Luckily, because of her English accent, she was vindicated.

Around the same time of the chaos, there was a man of God, a well-known prophet, who was working signs and wonders among the people. He was in a place that had the setting of a conference room, together with some people. He told them that he had commanded his body to grow taller, but they doubted him.

To put their doubting hearts to rest, he did something unimaginable, and they were stunned. He split himself into two, sending the other half of him to go and minister to the people on the other side of the room. As soon as the visions ended, Mwape came to this conclusion: the heavier the darkness, the greater the light. And the more the chaos, the greater the move of God such as no eye has seen nor ears heard.

The Twin Planets?

Again, in one of her visions, she saw planets, including one that closely looked like the earth - a twin planet to the earth. It was as though you could live on both planets. But there was something spectacularly different about this other earth. She saw a locked metal box that looked like a treasure box in between both planets. Then, it was like there were four major visible planets and others that were not as visible.

She entered a planet that looked different from the earth. It was a different time zone than the present day. It was as if she had travelled way ahead into the future. This vision may mean that other planets are liveable, only that there may be some time differences between one and the next.

There is a vital lesson to learn from Mwape's dreams. It is the certainty of the Lord's return. It is a wake-up call to the inescapable reality of the rapture and, more importantly, encouraging everyone to improve their walk with the Lord until the day comes. You will not know some things until you are privy to some special information that is only accessible when you have a deep-rooted relationship with God. And when God reveals his mind to his children, it is usually for a reason and at an appointed time. Therefore, we must align ourselves to His word and decree so that we will not be rejected when the day finally comes.

Food Shortage vs Price increase

Mwape saw that, something had happen and when everyone heard about it, the prices went up, a sandwich that would normally feed one person was sold at a price that would get you a food shopping for a week. And people still cued up to buy.

Africa

Mwape Saw a time of hardship coming, she saw nations struggling for money but they still went on building luxurious houses and even Africa looked good. It was about looking good as a whole. Then something happened like a destruction that was going to lead to people's captivity. Nevertheless, before that happened, she saw people looking for a prophet, for a man God was using, for salvation, and could not find any its either they were hiding or people could not tell who was who. As a result, people started guessing and went round asking different people saying are you the Anointed one, are you the man of God. And when they could not find any they started guessing in fear of perishing. Others started looking on maps to trying to locate were to go to fine men and women God was with.

Then they saw a Woman go in Labour and after that, she saw people being arrested to be used to fight. They fought their way out. Then someone that was once decent turned into a gangster on the streets. After all that, Mwape's friend that once persecuted them, went to Mwape and said.

"Mwape, i know that you are the one we are looking for... the anointed one," then she laughed reluctantly

Saying

We are not ignorant to this fact...

That we are ALL JOINT HEIRS WITH CHRIST.

Mwape's Late aunty was listening too and she asked her to say it again, then she repeated it as above. Meaning we are all children of God and all capable of seeking Him.

Then they were set free from looking for men of God knowing they also could reach God by themselves.

Chapter Summary

Signs suggest that we are approaching the end of the human race, technological advancement, corruption, social vices, and other evils. And these all point to the absolute certainty of the Lord's return.

You must maintain a daily Christian walk with God in order to avoid the inescapable tragedy that will befall the unrepentant sinners.

The Word of God is sure. If He has said it, it will happen no matter how long it takes.

Whatever you do, be prepared!

In the next chapter, you will learn...

That it is also possible for you to live a supernaturally normal life

What you must do to experience a divine relationship with God.

The benefits of walking with God and following Him wholeheartedly.

That prayer is a fundamental requirement to receiving and maintaining a powerful devotional life with God.

In the Christian journey, there are levels one must attain to be solidly grounded in faith.

Consistency in fellowship and practising the Word of God is the key to fulfilling the Word of God as a believer. "...But if any man draws back, my soul shall have no pleasure in him" (Hebrews 10:38).

CHAPTER EIGHT

You Too Can Receive This Experience

After Mwape's Coronavirus experience and her supernatural deliverance from it, she knew clearly within her that it was God or nothing. And since then, she has learned the true value of waiting upon the Lord. You see, that's the thing about receiving something from God, whether it be healing, a car, a house, or anything else. Sometimes you ask, and you receive. Be grateful for the privilege and ensure you maximize your received answers from the Lord by giving thanks. Sometimes too, the answer takes longer, but then, you must learn the art of patience, as the bible says in Isaiah 40:31.

"But those who wait on the Lord Shall renew their strength; They shall mount up with wings like eagles, They shall run and not be weary, They shall walk and not faint."

The thing is, the answers you seek don't show up as you expect them to because they come pre-packaged by God. If you're not discerning enough, you may miss your blessings.

Yielding herself to the Holy Spirit's leading has become Mwape's routine as it has been the only way to get ahead in life and through its challenges. There are times when the Holy Spirit would be teaching her the bible, and He would explain the intention behind the actions of the different biblical characters she was reading about. That way, she had a better understanding of the incident and had a proper grasp of the scriptures.

As a fashion designer, Mwape had enjoyed the fellowship of the Holy Spirit in more ways than one. Several times, she had run short of inspiration, thinking of innovative ways to make a garment or cut out patterns. And to her amazement, He would show her ideas in the form of a vision like a video tutorial. It is very possible to have this Bezalel gift since the bible tells us that there is no impossibility with God. Here is what the bible says in Exodus 31:1-5, 10,

"Then the Lord spoke to Moses, saying: 'See, I have called by name Bezalel, the son of Uri, the son of Hur, of the tribe of Judah.

"And I have filled him with the Spirit of God, in wisdom, in understanding, in knowledge, and in all manner of workmanship, to design artistic works, to work in gold, in silver, in bronze, in cutting jewels for setting, in carving wood, and to work in all manner of workmanship...

"The garments of ministry, the holy garments for Aaron the priest and the garments of his sons, to minister as priests."

There is more to God than priestly callings. You don't all have to be preachers or servers in church. Though it's good to participate, some are called to be assistants to Presidents, Prime Ministers, Kings, and Queens just like Daniel, Esther, and Joseph in the bible. The point is, you can serve God in your workplace or your everyday life. You don't have to be confined to a church setting before you can serve God.

Before teaching in a bible study, Mwape was sometimes unsure about which topic to teach her congregation. However, before starting, she'd ask the Holy Spirit for His leading, and He immediately released a topic for her to teach on. And usually, they were timely - a message people needed to hear for their current life situation. It's just like what Matthew 10:19-20 says, "But when they deliver you up, do not worry about how or what you should speak. For it will be given to you in that hour what you should speak; for it is not you who speak, but the Spirit of your Father who speaks in you."

There is one reason Mwape had been reluctant in going to a bible school or school of ministry. She wanted the youths to realize, just like the young prophet Jeremiah, God is still using and speaking to the young people and that you don't need to know it all to represent Him or for Him to use you.

You only need to love Him, as one of the FIF overseers once told Mwape. We always learn about His Love, but we don't talk much about loving Jesus. In John 21, Jesus asked Peter thrice if he loved Him. He wanted to ascertain the level of Peter's love for Him. Jesus understood that if you don't love Him sincerely, serving humanity will feel like you're in bondage or being used. And this is because just as the ministry of Jesus richly blessed them, they still killed Him. Thus, the same can happen to anyone who hangs his confidence on the superficial love of others that dissipates with time and circumstance.

You must have seen the most faith-filled, miracle-working men and women of God being severely persecuted. This is not to scare you but to simply prepare you so that you will not lose faith when the time comes.

Apostle Paul tells us to count it all as joy when we suffer persecution for our Lord Jesus's namesake. Why? Because you, being unworthy of redemption, now drink from the same cup as our Master and Saviour. Perhaps, you lack motivation because your fellows caused you to leave a church or faith. Here's all the encouragement you need, "Get back in faith first."

Remember that faith is no man's religion but God's, hence why the scriptures describe it as faith in God and not man. For as long as we see believers as gods, we will continue to stumble and fall because we are all not perfect. Thus says the Lord: "Cursed is the man who trusts in man and makes flesh his strength, whose heart departs from the Lord."

For those of you who feel hurt, realizing that you had placed your trust in men and not God, it's time to repent and ask God to heal you. Then ask him to fill you with His loving kindness. This will enable you to forgive and move beyond your past. Had Mwape not known that God heals our hearts, who knows where she would have been.

One thing is worthy of being noted. Mwape was never a perfect being, nor was she an angel. Despite her flaws, the Lord still chose to showcase His works through her. Obviously, His great love and mercy covered her and can cover you too. Are you worried to the extent that you feel unworthy and that you aren't good for anything? Not to worry. Mwape used to be like that too, but having a friend on the inside, like Jesus, who's able to teach you all things and help you rise above your challenges can make all the difference in your life.

To the rich, who think God is for the unlearned and the poor, that's a great mistake. You need his love, joy, and peace in the Holy ghost. The reason some celebrities get into drugs or rich folk commit suicide is that somehow, somewhere, they have lost their peace. This is not to say that poor people are always peaceful. No, poverty can lead you to sin outside God. However, the point is that we all need the Lord.

But then there is a question that has constantly arisen from Matthew 19:24, which says, "And again I say to you, it is easier for a camel to go through the eye of a needle than for a rich man to enter the kingdom of God." By this statement, Jesus meant that it would be difficult to enter heaven because of their reckless passion for acquiring more wealth than they can handle. The camel, on the other hand, in its simplicity and without any excess baggage, can easily find its way even if it's through the eyes of the needle gate. Note this, though. This is a metaphorical statement and not meant in literal terms, having a deeper meaning than just the rich and the poor scenario.

This, therefore, is a call to action for everyone who wishes to enter the kingdom of God to get rid of sinful characteristics. As the bible says in Galatians 5:19-21, "Now the works of the flesh are manifest, which are these; adultery, fornication, uncleanness, lasciviousness, idolatry, witchcraft, hatred, variance, emulations, wrath, strife, seditions, heresies, envying, murders, drunkenness, revelling, and such like: of the which I tell you before, as I have also told you in time past, that they which do such things shall not inherit the kingdom of God."

All these are attributes that constitute excess baggage that will hinder your easy access to heaven. So, you have to offload your baggage, repent, and don't try to walk in faith with heavy loads. Now, doesn't that also apply to poor people? Oh yes, it does! It applies to everyone who is not yet born again and anyone who hasn't accepted the Lord as his or her saviour. Having said that, to those that are saved yet struggle with the sins of the flesh, God is merciful. Simply ask for His help in your area of weakness. He is faithful!

And for those who are cautiously walking the paths of holiness, let us learn to serve the Lord rightly and arise to stand for him boldly as we bring in more harvest into the kingdom of God. As the bible says, "the harvest is plenty, but the labourers are few."

Now, for people that struggle to accept the saving faith of the Lord Jesus because they are struggling with homosexual dreams, or have friends or family that are in the LGBTQ+ community, or are convinced by orientation that they can be gay and Christian, the Lord still has a message for you.

For the past ten years, Mwape has been praying about it. And to conclude this book, she asked the Lord what she should say, and the Lord responded, He sent an angel that wore an off-white fitted suit. He stood just across the road, saying, "Tell the people what God has delivered you from 3 times." And He immediately disappeared.

But before that, around 2011, after meeting many beautiful hearted, gay men, Mwape was burdened for their salvation. Their community was fast gaining global attention and recognition that she wondered if there was a way for them to make heaven too.

So, she prayed about it, and the Lord responded to her in a vision. She saw herself in a gay village with a friend. While there, she entered a place that looked like a motel. And at its door were bouncers who were a fierce-looking black dog and a black cat. To be able to enter, a Dark cloud came upon her to hide her light in order not to draw attention. So she became like them. As soon as she gained access, she was put in a dark room, and the door was shut behind her. It was a dark room filled with a smothering blackness, and she couldn't find her way. Soon, she began to hear voices, although she didn't expect people to live in such a place.

So with her knowledge of the word of God, she called the light back by saying, "Let there be light." As soon as she had said that, a light appeared, and she gained her vision back. From where she stood, she could make out every activity going on there. Just then, she saw a pit with ladders inside, and people dug holes on different levels of the pit, signifying that people lived there. These people were frozen and had ice on their heads but didn't realize they were cold. So, the light that came brought warmth to them, and they realized where they were and asked for help. So she tried smuggling them out. And in the process, she woke up.

Many years after that, she had dreams of women wanting to sleep with her, as though she had turned gay too. She prayed fervently against it, but it did not easily go away. The dream reminded her of her early childhood circles. They were very perverse girls pretending to be husband and wife and sleeping together. Everyone wanted to try it then. As Mwape thought long and hard about it, she wondered if God was punishing her for her choice of friends in her past life, and if not, why? Surprisingly, in reality, she would look at women and wouldn't fancy them. So, that stirred a serious concern in her heart.

It did not occur to her that she was living the dream she saw in 2011. Then sometime in 2021, she saw a friend post a gay flag on Jesus. She talked with him as to why he felt gay people's enemies were Christians. Many other gay and non-gay people joined the conversation with over 70 comments to which she had to reply. One striking thing from their discussion was how they engaged positively and without any criticism. They did not attack her, nor did she, them. But it was educational from both sides. And shortly after that experience, she was burdened once again and had many questions that demanded answers like, "What happens to gay people that love the Lord and want to be Christian?" Then the Lord showed her another vision.

In the 1st dream, Mwape saw that she was involved with a certain girl, to the point of marriage. She was going to be a queen, and the whole world would have to witness that she was now a married lesbian.

As she put on her wedding dress, ready to go and meet her bride, she felt a conviction in her heart like a piece of stone. "Are you going to deny God for sexual pleasure?" It was a choice of loneliness versus fleshly satisfaction and the desire for having someone intimate in her life. But even at that moment, her love for the Lord was greater. Although Mwape was sad to let her down, she said to herself that she would rather have Jesus and be lonely than deny Him in public.

With that, she told people to tell her gay lover that the marriage was over. They later met and tried to settle their differences. But her gay partner wasn't ready to let her go. After much effort in futility, she decided to let Mwape follow her conviction and follow the Lord. Immediately, Mwape summoned the courage to turn her down. She felt all the affection fade away like smoke ascending into the heavens.

Then the dream continued. This time around, an angel commended her for not betraying the Lord for fleshly pleasure. The Lord also reminded Mwape that some homosexuals get the same conviction as she did yet deny Him privately before doing so publicly. And with that, she woke up.

As she sat on her bed, the dreams came flooding her mind once again. To think that she'd been carrying the burden for the gay community for almost ten years, and here, the Lord is saying He loves them just as much and that they too can enter the kingdom of God. However, it's subject to the condition of whether they accept Him or not as their Lord and personal saviour.

Now, You may not be homosexual, but you need to live inside God's designed plan for your life. You also need to encounter God's love and mercy before you can enter the kingdom of heaven. The truth is that God loves you regardless of how bad your past may have been or how terrible your present life is. All you need is to embrace the conviction that reminds you of the urgent need to start living according to the word of God and not according to your fleshly desires.

It is also dangerous to remain a lone-ranger as a new convert just learning the ropes of the Christian faith. You need a bible-believing church to anchor your faith solidly because it is important never to look back once you decide to follow Jesus. Additionally, you must grow in the knowledge of the word of God so that you will not be deceived again. God is interested in you. The question is, are you interested in the fellowship He is offering you? What will your answer be?

The bible says "Behold, I stand at the door, and I shall knock. If a man listens to my voice and opens the door, I will come in and eat with that person, and they with me" Revelation 3:20. The Lord is ready to come into your heart and make a home in you. As it's written in John 14:23. I pray you will respond to the call before it's too late. Someone thought they had tomorrow, and Covid-19 took them, another was taken by an accident, others thought it was just a headache, but it was so much more, and still others went to sleep and did not wake up. Why are you leaving eternity to chance? Why not invest now in a better future? You may have secured your children's financial future, but how about their afterlife? After all, this life is shorter than the afterlife. Your future is not death but everlasting life, as John 3:16b says. Whomsoever believes in Jesus Christ shall not perish but have everlasting life!

Now, this book is meant to show you the love of God and how God is very much interested in your everyday life. I prayed for the Lord to use this book to help answer many of life's questions. And I am glad that this book has proven to be a divine instrument used by God to reach out to those who are weak, helpless, Godless, and living without a life's purpose.

So, don't be too hard on yourself. It's okay to make mistakes but don't be limited by them. No one is perfect. It's understandable that you would have some struggles now and then, temptations, oppressions, challenges, and unpredictable situations. Yet, God's word remains infallible, our sure proof that He will be with us even in the most challenging conditions. Remember the fourth man in the fire with Shadrach, Meshach, and Abednego?

The story of Mwape is a great example of someone who rose from the ashes of self-aggrandizement, mediocrity, youthful exuberance, and wilfulness to be a shining light of hope to this generation and the ones to come.

Being wrapped around God's love is the only way to escape the ordeals and trials in the world today. There is no escaping it, considering the harsh realities we deal with every day. Just like Mwape later understood in life that it's either God or nothing, it's high time you drew near to God and watched your faith increase in these trying times.

If you would love to have the same kind of relationship with God on a personal level as Mwape did, say this prayer, "Lord Jesus, come into my life and be my Lord and my Saviour. Forgive me for all the sins I have committed knowingly and unknowingly. I believe that you died for me and that on the third day, you rose again.

"Help me live a holy life that will be pleasing unto you. Come and be my All in All. I surrender my life unto you so that you can have your way in me. I ask for the baptism of your Holy Spirit that I may be able to live a life led by your spirit. Thank you, Lord, for your mercy and love in Jesus' mighty name.

Amen."

Welcome to the kingdom of God. Now find a local, bible believing church or look for me. I will help you through as much as I can through Christ's power to stand for Him.

Chapter Summary

You can live the kind of life God wants you to if you allow Him to lead and direct you.

God loves you no matter how bad you think your life is. Just acknowledge that you need Him, and He help you through it all. There are some things you must do to live a supernaturally normal life. You must learn to pray, study the bible, and have fellowship with other believers to become a mature believer in Christ.

There are some things in life that you will struggle with, for as long as you don't get the message, like the Israelites who spent 40 years on a 5-day journey.

Remember how God told Hosea, a prophet, to marry a prostitute that kept living an indecent life even in marriage. The reason for that, was so that He could demonstrate how He feels when we worship Idols. We may never understand all things that God does, but all we can do is trust his goodness. He is faithful.

Conclusion

This is a story of a girl that came from humble beginnings, misunderstood by many to a point she blamed God for how life treated her.

We can all once in a while relate with her, but we also see how many times the Lord could have easily walked away from such a prideful soul that thought she could revenge God, but that's the thing, God, does not judge our actions but what's causing us to act as we do. How many times did Jesus answer people based on what was in their heart than what was actually said?.

So, incase there is someone out there that thinks they are too bad of a person to be Christian, you are the right person Jesus died for, at least you admit your wrongs. The most dangerous place to be is to sin and not know you are in the wrong, why because without conviction you can never repent.

So, as many as are willing to tell the Lord that, Lord, if you could use an empty tin, a person that struggles to speak, a person that struggles in many ways... if you can also fill me, though i be this empty tin, then here I am Lord, use me.

Jesus did not fellowship with his saints because they were perfect but because they knew they were imperfect and desired his perfection that can only happen with him being in you.

So, don't be hard on your self, take a deep breath, allow yourself to start again. Make a U-Turn. We have all made mistakes and made some U-turns. The thing about a U-Turn is, I remember coming from London from an Easter Conference and my battery died and my husband's phone lost connection, we made alot of U-turns, if it was on a normal road, a U-turn is not that bad but on a motorway, you really feel it... to a point I asked my husband to drive slowly so that, i could be reading the directions from the sign posts. So instead of 70mph into the wrong direction we slowed down. And eventually we did find our way, the point is, it's better to make a U-Turn now, than when you can't even remember your way back.

The Story of the prodigal son, reveals the Love of God, coming from a fatherless background Mwape could not relate with such love. We hear about how the father waits for you, as though one sat by the gate waiting for your return and yet you are the one in the wrong, like how does someone see you losing your way in sin and because you are about to fall into hell fire, he comes and takes the blame for you, so that we may realize that even in our mess he still Loves and cares about us. It's heart warming because, there is no such love on earth.

So, I pray this book may help you realize how valuable you are to God, and how much Jesus loves you, I pray today you open up your heart and embrace His love for you. So, if you are now born again, know that, it's not about just being a good Christian, just as the enemy the devil is recruiting an army that is creating an idol god, recently I saw another vision, were body parts / organs were being grown in this liquid thing like crops, scientifically great, I believe God allows it, but what are the intentions behind it.. Just as food can be good for you, but if abused can cause diabetes, or if expired can cause food poisoning, be wise when those times come. Always remember, you are also God's fiery Army and God's weapon. Jeremiah 51:20 Says,

"You are My battle-ax and weapons of war: For with you I will break the nation in pieces; With you I will destroy kingdoms;

To believers, let's work together as one body, the HARVEST IS INDEED PLENTY, but the laborers are few, as Matthew 20 says, let us realize, it's not about denominations but the souls. And helping each other as a body, is it not the bible in the book of James that said, only if we work together in love and peace will the world know that we are children of God.

Let us move past division, jealous and envy but each come together as one body in fellowship with Christ. Did we not learn anything about the good side of working together like those in Genesis 11:6 it says "And the Lord said, "Indeed the people are one and they all have one language, and this is what they begin to do; now nothing that they propose to do will be withheld from them." God himself said, nothing would be impossible if they Curry on in such oneness, such oneness is meant for us in the body of Christ, we have one language, the language of the bible and 1 great commission, win souls to the glory of His Holy name .

Dedication

To God be all the Glory!

I dedicate this book to my children and Hope - in heaven.

Dear Hope, me and your dad have never forgotten you. Though you didn't get to meet all these lovely people in our lives, you will meet them when our time comes to join you. We love you so much. When you see us shed tears for you occasionally, it's tears of joy, knowing you gave us hope, when we thought we could not have you... you were our hope that we could. So to me and your dad, you are still part of our family though not with us. Love you always.

Special thanks to Robert Owen my husband, thank you for being you, you've been my greatest source of motivation, i love you. And to all family, friends, Pastors and apostle, thank you for believing in me and pushing me to keep pursuing the Lord, thank you. To our children, I love you all so very much. You have taught me God's love for us and I am truly grateful to be called your mum. watching you grow is everything. To my beautiful siblings and friends Leonard, Hellen, Vera, Theresa, Charles, Racheal and Martha, my pillows where I rest my head, thank you oO.

Last but not the least, my mum, thank you for raising the bar so high for us, you are forever our inspiration, thank you for not giving up on us. We love you like a cup of tea x. And to my Beautiful in-laws, the Owens, you are the best in-laws one could ever wish for, Love you so much.

Since am not able to list everyone down, to you, yes you, thank you for being my best friend, thank you for the joy and happiness you brought in my life. You made my life beautiful, I wish you all my very best in your lives too.

Contact or Follow Me and subscribe...
for Mentoring and Empowerment
Email:godsfieryarmy@gmail.com
Facebook: Victoria Owen vkwise or Gods fiery Army
TIKTOK:: @godsfieryArmy
YouTube : God's Fiery Army

www.ingramcontent.com/pod-product-compliance
Lightning Source LLC
Chambersburg PA
CBHW071536080526
44588CB00011B/1689